Introduction......

I believe writing is one of the most relaxing things to the mind as far as imagination goes, so as I wrote and continue to write these poems that I more consider to just be my thoughts I feel as if I'm giving the readers one of the most personal gifts one person can share with the next person and that is a peek into the way I think secretly as well as the in depth explanations of my thoughts.
I mean really.... What's more intimate and mind blowing than going into the thoughts and feelings of another person? I have shared some of the most beautiful things of my life and how I saw them and continue to see them as well as some of the most heartbreaking and saddening things of my life but I do all of this as a gift to the world of readers and deep thinkers ....I beg of you ,enjoy my work ,let it spark the types of conversation that is most memorable to your minds, hearts and souls.
       Sincerely,
        Shahid Boone

A Fieldhand's Prayer

Alhamdulillah...I thank God
I thank my lord for the favors and blessings he bestows upon me, to this I have no problem confessing...I'm thankful for these eyes ,ears and tears ..
    for this bright mind being able to see life ohhhhhhh so clear ..
    I am thankful for every second of every moment of every year I spent up there sexually frustrated driven to the point of acknowledging that I too masturbate ...WAIT WAIT WAIT
You see ,what it is that I'm trying to articulate is that even life's toughest moments didn't really prove to be worthy opponents
    cause I'm still here fighting until the blissful end (inshallah) lord willing ...
    I thank my Rubb (my lord) for the blessings spilling into my cup ...in my observation it's easy in today's world to become a pessimist , just take a quick look at this election ish (it looks like a bad movie) So I remain humble and allow for life's simpler things to move me and I'm not hinting in which direction I'm headed cause you should already know ...
    I'm thankful for the youthful people I am allowed to love and their reciprocation was an indication that I could make a difference out here so I packed up all my fear and pulled out every ounce of bravery and started attacking today's new wave of slavery...
    I thank Ar-Rahman ,the one who owns mercy ...for giving me life of mind and not making me blind and when I say blind I don't mean sight I mean vision
    It's in my wisdom that I see how most of y'all give life to suckerish feelings while I instead allow for my multiple successes to suffocate it then I hide and relocate it so none of you can try to resuscitate it, the youthful minds are frustrated because they feel as if no one understands their plights so they lose their sights in opiate induced hazes and then die trying to find a way through the ghetto's deadly mazes
    They just trying to get out ,wondering if it's less stress in their deaths,so yesssss even until my very last breaths .....I will thank my lord

AmeriKKKa's Honesty

In the USA I'm a resident so I wanna start this off by personally sending a shoutout to my president for making the status of racism in this country so evident and anyone who can't see this new wave of slavery has to be viewing it lazily ,as if the similarities are alarming....

A single call from a white person will have the law swarming ,wrapping our wrists ......sorta like they used to wrap their necks and is it me or did it take that Nike ad for all black athletes to say they were willing to take a knee wit Colin Kaepernick ?

If you look at the past and look at the present, can you tell me what hasn't happened yet?

you see , the truest form of their hypocrisy is that this country in itself was built off of all types of apothecary and that's what proves the racism to be flagrant ,because the moment when we started trying it ..it became a life sentence so it's like this house is fucked up from the roof to the basement (pay attention) can I mention how we went from enslavement to our parents gobbling up that spoon full of poison from president Reagan ,to nowadays it seems to be that our flavor is their main cravin ? EVERY TIME I TURN ON THE TV I see a middle aged white person black ppl waving and that's a helluva statement yet true

So now we all begin to see the loss that disconnect can cost ....there's a whole generation prepared to be lost ,cause they got em on percs a plenty , henny and newports plus the cops shooting at these lil niggas like it's a new sport...... We know how to hold our tongues in check ,yet their abandonment had us lose respect and go directly at the necks of older blacks because they so quick to discredit us ....but never learned to point them same fingers at the ones who labeled their children super predators , see y'all probably thought this was a thing bout republicans versus Democrats but I'm really a Crackhouse kid so believe when i say "we ain't into that " and since we on the subject , no need to wonder what I'm hinting at , I'm speaking of Ms Clinton and her cold ass HER HUBBY....President Clinton got head in the Oval Office,smoked weed and played jazz on a sax and if you think back you'll remember that's what made him damn near universally accepted by the blacks ? (but they never noticed who he was sending to jail never to be comin back?)We only workin wit the facts (SHOUTOUT ARKANSAS) thennnnnn they say we fell in love wit president Obama because he was black and while never mentioning how he dropped osama

Friend MY protector and depression set in and loneliness was in abundance hurt more than ever desolate and tears were uncontrollable I was inconsolable it was wicked facing that pain alone in prison and I wasn't smart enough so I began to question my Lord's wisdom (subhanallah) but listen y'all you gotta understand I never went thru anything remotely close to this and now I'm free and my heart wants see you and bid off of the secrets we shared and all the fun times but I can't so I will cry in the dark and let the confidence of my smiles cover my heart's sting I just had to let them know.......Brothers Remember Everything
I love you Mark

BROWN SUGAR RUSH

Hey Mahogany it's my sanity that you're robbing me of ,your ebony eyes shaped like almonds full of seduction my power is full of reduction steadily reducing infatuation and producing love my mind wanders into far off places ...when I think of you I envision Parisian nights Vietnamese mornings and Dubai days the ways in which your hips sways leaves me in a daze the strength of this woman should be praised and lauded fuck that you should be applauded your steps are graceful and elegant your movements are tasteful and is that Chanel cause I'm smellin it ? Your voice is melodic and almost hypnotic to the point that I must confess sometimes I fall into the sound and forget the topic as a matter of fact your skin is the most luscious of brown your lips are full of the type of kisses that've had men drown in them I'm a willing victim who's fallen in love with your venom.... oh silly me , i willingly open my neck and say "ay .bite me again"

Chamber of Champions

Sitting here listening to meek talk bout wins and losses ,has me noticing ,horribly relayed messages from the pen got us comin home tryna figure out how the winners took so many losses is proof these lames came home before us fraudin ,twisting the truth , misleading the youth tricked y'all into callin em bosses ,not knowing that they were the Judas sent back meant to double cross us THIS IS PHILADELPHIA where it's best to warn the kids wit cautions before allowing em to leave the doorsteps turned on the news -another kid was just shot the smell of death ☐ scented by gunpowder and blood ,shit sickening ,it got me nauseas , they told y'all they was tryna cake huh, but ain't tell y'all it was all crumbs on they topping ,and y'all all bums we ain't stopping all they slickest moves I'm out here out foxing I'm the missing WU member ... I was upstate physically & mentally shadowboxin ,figured out what to master once I got home and saw how easily y'all fall slave to desire ,time to remix the dream ,so i jumped back in the kitchen and went back to whippin the cream, I'm the product of a distant dream ,Marcus on a rainy day he probably had on grainy grey or maybe even minty green as he allowed his mind to absorb the absurdness of the scene ,societal mistreatment towards his kith and kin and just in case y'all should ever be wondering or lookin , I'll probably be somewhere in solitude smokin weed ,shedding tears over unjustified murders of women ,children & men of my hue ,because these types of things truly does pain me the lack in public outrage has me asking ,how exactly does it affect you?

DR KING'S NIGHTMARE

　　Listen i told these lames I'm switchin lanes I learned all my lessons from the game that crack taught ,Im the dirty gangster's version of Black Thought ,a hard hearted Black Dante ,grew up in North Pompeii... Ohhhhhhhh my wordplay .....that'll leave you fighting a slight bout of wooziness especially when I allow for my mind to erupt ... mt Vesuvius .... I just been tryna figure out how today's beggars became the choosiest , and kids manners nowadays are the goofiest maybe because the parents either fear the children that they bore or just don't care bout their actions as long as they get a nice cut off their next score and these be the same ones falling all over the floor when they hear their babies don't exist no more and since black folk don't got time to ensure that their households are fully insured , well ,burial bout to be the first thing they see they can't truly afford ,so now public begging is the chore , gofundme..fish frying,poor seeking help from the poor but I guess I'm just corny boul who got fake awake doin damn near two decades upstate ...we as black ppl got a whole lot on our plate and I'm just hoping to god we aren't really satisfied with all this fake accepted as real and the real being so fake ...like why is is it so hard for y'all to love yet so easy to hate ? I only speak on things that interests me ...you see, I was upstate ,i remember it vividly,being in the hole only human interaction was the nigga in the next cell , I'm free now ,I'm in the car on my way to the next sell born on the highway to hell , I grew up in the fast lane ,lately been shedding tears thinking of past pains ,paying for champagne wit blood money reminiscing over everything these streets done took from me ,you see I'm from the place where death kisses you on the forehead ,this is PHILLY our headlines been crazy like 5 shot ,4 dead it's nothing to see one legged dope fiends who never knew what hope means ,young niggas got coke dreams ,prison nightmares were birthed right here ....it smells like burnt crack and hidden rat fear out here ,im from where convicts come up wit the illest inventions , I got a question to mention " If niggas is on angles why are you even in their dimension to give them something to mention ?"
Believe in yourself allow your presence to bring oxygen to the hemisphere "Mannnnn Og niggas ain't tryna hear this shit out here   !" ....youngin clip so long it ain't a stick ...it resembles a spear ...when they hit you they get generous and leave you the spares , these Kings were birthed in despair and taught that nothing is spared & life ain't fair so if they hit you cause you was bluffing ...that shits fair and watch who you standing wit cause they cop bodies by the pair like a fresh

pair of air Jordan's ... heartbreaking ...shortie out here whorin for the next nigga lookin important ,asking questions about which flights he boarding because abuse to her life is domestic so she seeking to go foreign ,y'all looking like the lost grandchildren of Lauryn so I'm telling Ms Hill they need another dowop cause they all stuck on that thing and Lil homie can't understand the violence the streets bring if he out here rolling on a bean cause the killers rolling wit assault rifles and some of em wearing a beam , I'm from the ghetto aka Willie Lynch's dream and the reality of that one thought can make the conscious of a true black man cry and scream ....everybody gotta feel this right here , I'm just hoping against hope that we wake up from Dr King's nightmare

Eyes of Resuscitation

I definitely dedicate my efforts to my kids
I'm So tired of corny shit getting by ,
so,first things first pull
up a chair
wise discussions between gangsters always start wit statements like "let's just be fair "
I'm a grown ass man I get fresh , stay fly
y'all we cats are fleek
I'm really from the street,grew up dirty /more than a couple crooked teeth ,my mind is filthier than Brewster's millions, I'm devoid of feelings the heart in my chest is empty ....similar to a trash can in a Crackhouse full of waste from immoral acts taking place in the back of a two bedroom flat in the middle of nowhere,my heart died right there oddly it came back to life when I looked into her little eyes and understanding that we are now forever part of each other's lives makes me thankful for the epic failures I've seem to have survived praying that all of the things I've been through is what will help me shield you from the evils of this planet of morons... Im gon wait til I see your intellect kick in and tell you to look up and pick which cloud you wanna soar on and hold conversation more on how to be patient with the ppl but never lie to yourself about the snakes in your life that are see through ,make sure your friends see you & love you and appreciate how you just be you , from the time your mom had you , you had me , I undertake this task gladly cause my dead heart gains new life and light when I hear my babies call me daddddddddyyyyyy

Eyes Wide Shut

It's a new day.... humility just murdered hubris , but be careful because hubris also has the ability to murder humility... i got some stuff on my mind to share so hopefully y'all feeling me ....I wanna start by saying first , i feel so blessed to be free and in all of your presence , feeling like the chosen one to speak for the iron backed peasants , to be recognized as one of the guys who can vocalize the proverbial pointed finger at the malfeasance of our justice system, if we look at past presidents as evidence that Donald Trump is a excellent caricature of all that's wrong with lady America's character , then wouldn't we have a helluva conversational piece to start with ? The problem is that it seems like white ppl been gaining their info from airwaves when y'all should be tuned in and listening to the sounds of the streets maybe then you'd understand that our lives really aint that sweet ,you see,what it is that I'm trying to discern is what exactly do whites concern themselves with as human rights, i mean damn y'all do see us as humans ,right? So how all y'all ain't go up in arms when lil Tamir Rice lost his life ? He was a kid in a park playing wit a toy gun .... i guess it's true ,it doesn't hit home as hard when he doesn't resemble the son playing in your front yard ,but, we ain't have no white picket fences like Dennis who was so bad in fact he was referred to as a menace but they never stopped to think of putting that child in a prison , they said stick to facts leave the rappers to create the fiction…..but but but wait cause I'm not finished ..... church ☐ shooting Ass Dylan got burger king when he finished his business , but Mr Garner got choked out cause he chose to make loosie selling his business... what type of sickness is this when Philadelphia & Chicago streets are running red like a marathon of women all on their menses , we gotta go back to using plain old common senses i be talking but it seems like no one listens , i feel as if I'm trying to convince the convinceless to go against their conventions and change them mental conditions because bad decisions lead to weaker actions ,so now we ALL on parole or probation across the nation that's how they leaving us defenseless .....yeah man I'm paying attention and I'm just sayin a lot of this shit is senseless #whatsgoinon

FAMILIAL ADVICE

I've been through some things in life, so,
My advice is slow down on the stressin
you'll find your answers to the things in your life that are questions if you pay closer attention to the lessons ,and don't just count em ,store away them blessings in this world where blacks are placed in a position of surviving like wild peasants ...

 they on the news outraged by your crimes but place disclosures on their malfeasance, the key to prison is payment for our presence ,so black kids get served up like Christmas presents my mind was shaped and engineered by legends and that may be too much for you to handle cause most are heavier drinkers than they are thinkers and that's Joe as shit (how joe?)...
That shit joe camel , joe too cool calari ... this vintage game homie we talkin coleco vision & Atari,swimming with sharks you fake tough guys get exposed as calamari y'all octopussy so don't push me cause i swear to god you'll be sorry me and this gun of mine got a 007 type bond ,cut you into short time ....I've watched with my eyes at least 5 good guys blood spill cause they chose to shine and chill in the city of slime ,
   Me & my friends were born way beneath the poverty line ,tricked into believing that you only live as good as the seriousness of the types of crimes you've been committing ....but it's a setup so I'm here begging y'all to sit still and think of ways to do things different ,there's a huge difference between living and existin and trust me you don't wanna find yourself in that grey area called prison ....dawg this ain't superstition .... it's actually a few words of wisdom from a person who fell under 15 years of their supervision

FELONIOUS BEHAVIOR

Wherever the liars hide , that truth gon find ya
And I'm guessing y'all need a reminder cause I see a bunch of people done caught amnesia... so I'm back and I'm bout to get it shaking like I just had a couple seizures, I'm dropping shit so fly it could probably only best be described as bird fèces , truth is they watched me struggle for years ask em about me and i bet they still wouldn't produce an honest thesis, so imma share wit y'all one of my many secrets ... I got a whole heart in my chest...it's just been broken into a thousand pieces, so I shower alone to hide the tears letting the water wash over my features I'm just a different type of creature , I couldn't start wit the yelling and screaming ,cause frankly,it just ain't me...I'm reporting Fresh from the north side of philly

I call it the city of snake pits , cause this is where niggas is into openly accepting fake shit ,

so we can't even slow down cars to speak to em past the basics it's the blind leading the blind botched lasics and

I ain't gon lie ....Philly is one of the livest places on earth
it's also the type of place where you can meet niggas who's mom, his babymom mom and the baby mom all strung up on percs...that shit hurts cause it's laughable ,but not funny ....I walked through some dark nights to ensure my daughters' days stay sunny & I travel trying to intellectually link up with ppl of like minds who ain't got no time to be trying to waste time beefing over what was posted on some weirdo's timelines ...you see , guys like me grew up in the middle of a whirlwind of waste baskets, and mishandled crack flips had my money fucked up , and since i don't know how to Ass kiss these niggas had me out here doin gymnastics.... all backflips Jay Z said we all lose when the family feuds but I be feeling like what do I got to lose when i paid my dues and these dudes still won't support my views ,yet when my name is mentioned they'll use negativity to fuel their kids food for thought

And I only learned that last part when the gavel dropped in court

(prison is a solitary fight that's fought)

around then i began to relearn all the life lessons I was ever taught and this what I come up with :

If your survival is of virtue then never allow the squares into your circle cause I swear to God that shit'll hurt you

Look at me ... A Nigga life like his body ... so scarred...

so I learned to ignore fuckery ,focus on the numbers and run up the bag .... goyard...

Y'all niggas been out here breaking the law living y'all life in inches explaining it upstate ... that's the whole yard .

  while we been running the streets like it's a marathon ...Hugh Hef the way i bring bunnies out ☐ when I got them carrots on ... got em walking by switching asses releasing pheromones... but my heart colder than children's broken spirits growing up on the crack scene ... I don't think y'all understand what I mean ,

     i was out here drying clean dirty clothes for school on heaters fueled by kerosene..

     and now y'all wanna pay to hear what you've never cared to have seen? That's obscene heartbreaking the way blacks carrying themselves like pigs , yes the characteristics of slothenous animals , speaking irreverently, acting unintelligently and because I sold dope and shot some niggas I'm forever a bad guy is what you're telling me ? Even though now Netflix subscriptions got y'all witnessing how this system been failing me ... i guess y'all can't understand the picture from my angle , it takes two to tango and we got all the rhythm but still dancing to them white ppl melody ... I remember hearing "STAND FOR SOMETHING OR FALL FOR ANYTHING " look y'all fell for everything and that my nig .....that's truly the felony

Fibers of Character

In today's world my character is a rarity
In yesterday's news my tears gave me clarity
In tomorrow's sunrise ,should i survive I'll probably surprise and give forgiveness as a charity....but At no point in my life's future will I ever allow for anyone's negativity to disparage me in pursuit of my achievements , I see what's going on out here so I'm working hard tryna give these kids something to believe in ,they've been trapped in a liars' audience captivated by fraudulence ,deceived by men who sold them big money Sonny dreams all the while transforming em into burnt down fizzled out ignorant lil fiends ..... they need to know it's not cool to be fiends or junkies ,glorifying incarceration with bunkies snaking each other in pursuit of some money ,nor is it acceptable to make your home life neglectable , look like we got a laundry list I'm tryna reach out to Lil sis and let her know it's not ever gon be okay to refer to herself as a bad bitch ,but you see , she feels superior because she holds scalpels while doctors perform surgery...she's entrusted to protect incisions,staples and stitches .... you better than that and as a matter of fact I need you to make better decisions ...you should seek to own the institutions where they seek positions .... sadly my intuitions tells me there'll never be another Martin, Malcolm or Ali and unlike a lot of y'all that's just not fine by me....

    In conclusion I wanna ask a question , it's really completely off topic , but i been watching and this is quite toxic so maybe if I speak on it we can put our heads together and try to figure out how to stop it .... here's the question : Why do black ppl become so angry over white collusion, but the moment any of you gain some type of inclusion you quick to ask the next black through the door "WOWWWW who dafuq let you in ?"

Fit The Description

Hey y'all come here and gather around give me a a lil bit of your attention so I may mention a conversation you
may have heard and you tell me if it's real life or fiction it's called ...you fit the description
It was a beautifully sunny autumn day you know the type that makes you lift some prohibitions and say "aww let em play!" Makes you not wanna drive so you decide to walk today only to hear someone pull up and say "hey buddy where ya headed?" You turn and notice it's someone so dreaded...THE POLICE!

Me: headed to the store (lookin at this menace)
Him: come here let's talk for a few minutes(he's lookin like don't try me)
Me: (lookin like why me?) for what? About what? I'm busy got some place I should be
Him: come here let me see some I.d and where you going that's so important?
Me: (as I hand him my I.d)I'm going to the pharmacy to fill my baby's prescription
Him: (with his hand on his pistol reaching for my I.d) ok just great ....but we got a problem cause you fit the description
Me: of who? Doing what? (nasty feeling in my gut)
Him: robbery of two women
Me: (chuckles nervously) and just so happens the robbers look like me?
Him: (sarcastically) yeah but you can be done and through if you agree to let me put these cuffs on you and take a ride to let the victims see
Me: (looking him squarely in the eyes I say) no how! no way ! Unh unh not today! I dont agree and if I'm not under arrest then why is it me that you must detain I thought Lincoln done away with slavery so why you so quick to try to put me in chains ?
Him: listen buddy just stand here (he's getting angry)
Me: how is this any of my concern I work to feed my family until my muscles ache and my eyes burn
Him: I'm sure you do just stay calm remain patient and this'll all be done and through and you'll be free to go do you as y'all say
Me: (as y'all say? Let it go bro) yeah whatever where are they then cause I'm innocent

Him:(giggling) this time....
Just then another cruiser arrived and to my surprise a young woman and man were let out by the police officer but didn't he say it was two women? He's looking at me grinning but both looked and said "no it wasn't him"
Him: sorry for the delay of your day but you gotta understand my apprehension cause we both know you fit the description

FRIENDLY ADVICE

Have you ever sat and asked yourself about your happiness?

Like why is it that those closest treat us the crappiest?

Don't be alarmed this isn't a pointed BOMB towards anyone in particular but it's an observance that's been a deep pain like a shot to the testicular area and ask any man they'll say that's the worst .... But anyway let's get back to this opening verse......

people rarely realize their reaction is the proof of their guilt, so when I say my thoughts aren't a tirade towards the takers but rather a reminder for the givers ,that snakes don't bark nor chirp (naw ,they just slither and strike)

Ever notice how ppl tend not to celebrate your accomplishments like they enjoy watching your failures ?

For instance could you call five friends and come up with rent money if need be? But aren't they the same ones that say "I'm here if you need me?"

We've become accustomed to walking in the dark alone but it's a lot less scary when you have a friend along

we just have to choose to cut off the takers cause they're nothing more than up close haters and get in the game wit some real life players, you know the type that really keep you in their prayers and tells you shrug off all naysayers

My advice is to take some time out of your life and go get you a real friend and try your hardest to be a real friend back

It's really as simple as that

G.P.A
Greatest Poet Alive

I'm a poet , I say that out loud so everyone can know it, I'm a street professor who wanna check the g.p.a . (grade point average?) I'm the greatest poet alive and I'm prepared to prove it so I'm gon give it to y'all in every line until everybody lose it .... my wordplay so Ill it's gon have y'all wondering why I ain't tryna get into music Cause I'm still tryna find a beat hard enough to tell these young niggas that that street beef real deep like best friends bodies being found wit no head ,hands or feet   yeah this street life real sweet like poison ☠ ▢ sprinkled all over cereal and i swear to god every pistol I ever touched i never saw a serial ...my mind is fly so naturally my view point is aerial and my vocab is imperial to you peons you won't get the repetitive redundancy that you've come expecting to see ...naw ...not right here ... not with me ,not tonight .... I'm the unofficial son of Sonja Sanchez asking real questions like ayyy it don't seem wrong to you that y'all out here doin everything them racist ppl say well those are things niggers are just prone to do ? I know as some of y'all listen your mind like dis mfer spittin got you sayin this what's been missin so where dafuq you been ..then I have to reply Just got home from prison , so glad I made the decision to move independent, i notice nowadays the so-called thoroughbreds be dope dépendants mannnnnnn listen it's been a lot of street sinnin and not enough gangster repentin ...y'all niggas say you can read between the lines but never learned to write a sentence when a nigga got sentenced but came home to find out y'all damn sure been signing them statements I be having nightmares of my babies seeing my face in my homies pendants nigga like me got to the top by inches, centimeters ,millimeters and kilograms now when I slide through they whisper " there he go he the man" snakes slither tryna shake my hands I just want y'all to heed the advice man understand blood is the price the streets demand and respect is what we command Boi I'm gangster by more than chance grew up without a father or a belt cold hearted but I made sure I had a pistol in my pants and since i come directly out the crackhouse I have the humility of immigrants coming from 3rd world countries , with the anger of child soldiers who grew up never sober until I found myself on the next episode of young dumb and caught wit a buncha baking soda.... ay man this nigga look like judge Mathis basically just said it was over ... snatched 15 winters PLUS THE summers you'll never know how many nights I sat up and daydreamed about big butt bitches sittin on the hoods of Benzes and hummers surrounded by real life killers & young gunners but them old heads took notice that I had more than numbers & a pie factory running in my mind ,so they started showing me different things ...like ,let my first investment be my time ,allow my mind to be my grind and then I noticed it was only my body that was doing that time .... Im a real nigga wit real homies that say cuz some say bruh I got some wild Ny niggas that scream slime and I even know a cool ass MS13 gamgbangin Mexican nigga named 2-9 and I ain't the worst motherfucker in the world but I been to the hole more than a few times so after all that y'all know it be killing me tryna wrap my mind around how everybody ballin and shooting out here like Harden but the kids still starvin look like y'all fell for all them tricks you silly rabbits amd these drug habits got y'all not even noticing the streets are mister mcgregors garden , came home wondering what's going on like Marvin ,tryna figure out how to help the future like Garvey but past betrayal still scars me and the streets stay in touch trying to call me they think I still got it they on my line sayin y'all all moving garbage the streets gon always love me but don't ask these lyin ass niggas, naw ask the smokers , they gon say you now locked in wit the illest villain since Heath decided to play Joker ☐ I write about Drug dealing Draconian nights how the streets stole our souls , replaced our dreams with nightmares of kilo goals I'm Bram Stoker streets ... I don't speak for the new Oprahs this for field hands still eating cornbread and fried okra shedding tears ova young boys dying in the field brainwashed into hopin to be big as Sosa .... that's actually a dream in a country where black men still getting shot in they homes   on they sofas dangerously eating ice cream .....REWIND HIT EM WIT THAT ONE ONE MORE TIME ... then lemme say that one more time I don't speak for the y'all new Oprahs , this for the field hadnds still eating cornbread and fried okra shedding tears ova young boys dying in the field brainwashed into hopin to be the new Sosa .... that's actually a dream in a country where black men still getting shot in their homes   on their sofas dangerously eating ice cream ... dangerously eating ice cream... I'm the greatest poet alive that's what I scream .I'm the greatest poet alive that's what I scream

GENERATIONAL WILLIES

They think parental crackhouse inhalation haunts us but if we gon be truly honest, I'm more vexed that y'all don't see they looking past us to those behind us tryna have them learn life from a position of prison, earning stripes showing contrition steadily convincing a buncha dishonest ppl they've labeled as your honors they pay the rappers to live lives that propagate them carrying them llamas ... y'all niggas chasing commas but the commas they gon give ain't in the bank I'm telling y'all now it's served up in the holding tank , I've dealt with DA's that've tried to put fear in me , quick question : you ever endured a year of diesel therapy ?

My nigga I'm he link between society and the clink I'm Americas' dirty lil secret ...real life crack house kid , double digit prison bid , shot everywhere except for the left leg ,my heart or my my wig , so you can't truly expect me to listen to a person telling me what they think it is While most ppl have a lot of fucked up moments in their life I feel like I've suffered through the most consecutive seconds of being the consecutive second knowing I should be the primary I've yet to meet a person who's been through as much and still allows for the mind to vary from very morbid and sordid to spitting some shit that will have your girl screaming my name like NORBIT .... sadly earthlings worship stars while intellectuals praise the mindsets that are set for a different orbit or solar systems, dripped in wisdom from old cats destined to die in prisons it was their unnurturing intervention that stopped the interventionist's visions of me so whenever I speak of them it will be from a place where they will always be above me ,cause they showed me how to love me so even when everyone screams they wanna be a rap god , I'm like "nah I'm cool with just being a regular ass cool black guy" ….and that's ok

GUILTY DISCRETION

I love our conversations because they never contain " did you hear bout so and so & such and such " ...... I'm so sarcastic and she's witty as fuck ,
we get together and we focus on us ,
she finds herself trapped in my clutch, losing herself willingly to my touch ,she's been wondering if I know when enough is enough ..
but I don't ....
so she secretly hopes I'll stop before we wind up taking it there ..
but I won't ...
she calls and I don't answer I just pull up talking like Big Worm (like) GURL WTF YOU WANT ?!

She's the sexy chocolate girl wit the fly spirit... her frame reminds me of an unsang Sadé lyric , I wanna bite her here ,kissing her there making her say my name so loud that the neighbors can hear it ... lately she's really been turning me on , is that part apparent?

I've been having thoughts of stroking her until we both go incoherent flipping her over ,going deep til I'm swimming meanwhile in this picture she's face down biting on the linen , we're more than mere men and women,the definition of mythical creatures, I tell her leave the lights on cause I wanna see all these features , now could you possibly visualize the look in his eyes as he kisses behind your knees ,working his tongue up your inner thighs til he reaches his prize ,then taking you for a hard ride ... these guys ,they try turning you on with money (how funny) my words make you call me Mr Boone mental stimulation leaving you wetter than water balloons ...

treat my mind like your personal escape room and the artist in me will treat your body like a personal canvas as you wrap your ankles around my back I'll whisper in your ear there's no place like home ,then keep digging like I'm searching for Kansas, I'm the fire to your ice , we can use this bed as a conduit we meet in seclusion and fuck til we come to every conclusion ....biting and licking until you produce my favorite fluid ,I been waiting for your sassy ass to tell me ACT LIKE NIKE NIGGA AND JUST DO IT you got me at the right moment (gone on The henny) should've caught me sober cause now I'm definitely fucking you over just licked my fingers now wanna sip from your fountain you got me harder than the side of mountains that's boulder ... and I'm getting bolder ,body heat so high it'll smolder , placing knees to shoulder making you take it all like a soldier until it's over ... next time you wanna bone all you gotta do is look out your window & say HEEEEEERE ROVER

Heartbreak of a Deadbeat Dad

I have to say I'm truly astonished at the lack of their being admonished for being so dishonest ...

You know ...

boy meets girl and plays the role to get what he wants then turns cold and she's confused cause she didn't even know she was a game more the less part of his cheat code , and his old heads laugh saying "the game is sold not told"...

Until it's your daughter that's old enough..
Yeah old enough to be told she's tough and the crazy part is SHE IS tough! .....

One of the most beautiful creatures to walk this earth but you weren't there to teach her what she was worth cause you were too busy painting the town...
now ....

it's coming back that your baby-girl your princess is out here doing things to tarnish and taint her crown.......

Now you ready to go gung-ho but you start thinking about what you done tho and start to wonder is this that BITCH KARMA teaching an unwanted lesson?

or is this the BEAUTY OF KARMA showing you that what went around came around , pulling the mirror to the face of a bum ass clown letting him know he is just a crumb pretending to be a king with no crown........ sooooo speaking for all the hardworking baby mamas .....duckin baby daddy drama....

In the famous words of my man Marty-Mar "MANNNNN SIT YO DUMBASS DOWN!"

Heartbreak of a Crackhouse Kid

He tells himself she loves me ....but she burns and beats me and calls me names ,she plays with my head ,takes me thru games of the mind shattered dreams ,broken hearts and flowing tears created a bond forged thru fears

    her voice weakens knees when heard by our ears ....QUESTION : Have you ever smelled the skin of a three year old as it sears on a old project stove? Oh my ..... look at the wicked web this snake has wove ...

    she's despicable and very unpredictable,   punches to the face ,kicks to the abdomen and beatings with a steel rod had me sitting in contemplation wondering if there's really even a God (subhannallah) that means exalted is the lord ...but y'all gotta understand it's a hard thing to comprehend as a kid watching my blood flowing openly onto the kitchen floor .... this is the part of the poem where i usually tell ppl close their eyes and when they close them I tell em to close them a lil tighter open their minds a lil wider   and try to hear the crunch of the pliers coming down on the fingers of a 7year old ... When the one entrusted to teach us to love teaches us to harm then the fire alarm should be pulled ,cause it is a blaze that'll burn for days ,weeks ,months and decades now the same person shows a fackad or I meant to say facade it be blowing my mind , i find it fairly odd that this chick actually has the audacity to say she's fearing of God but, from her secret pulpit all she preaches is bullshit ...separation ,partisanship, and hate so if you think I should learn to love the monster I come from ... i guess will just bow my head in shame and say "its too late ....cause I'm already damaged goods "

or .... this is the part of the poem where i usually tell ppl close their eyes and when they close them I tell em to close them a lil tighter open their minds a lil wider   and try to hear the crunch of the pliers coming down on the fingers of a 7year old ... When the one entrusted to teach us to love teaches us to harm then the fire alarm should be pulled ,cause it is a blaze that'll burn for days ,weeks ,months and decades now the same person shows a facade or I meant to say facade it be cracking me up how this woman actually has the audacity to say she's fearing of God but, from her secret pulpit all she preaches is bullshit ...separation ,partisanship, and hate so if you think I should learn to love the monster I come from ... i guess will just bow my head in shame and say "its too late ....cause I'm already damaged goods "

ld ... When the one entrusted to teach us to love teaches us to harm then the fire alarm should be pulled ,cause it is a blaze that'll burn for days ,weeks ,months and decades now the same person shows a facade or I meant to say facade it be

cracking me up how this woman actually has the audacity to say she's fearing of God but, from her secret pulpit all she preaches is bullshit ...separation ,partisanship, and hate so if you think I should learn to love the monster I come from ... i guess will just bow my head in shame and say "its too late ....cause I'm already damaged goods
I am sitting thinking of a word ......
audacious is the word I'll use to describe how appalled I am that y'all done openly accepted this fake shit ....

   for those of you who don't understand "finessing" is snake shit I would know what it is cause I grew up in a snake pit

  I recently had my heart broken when learned my brother feels some type of way cause I got snake bit I swear y'all gotta chill wit the hate shit ,

    yet sadly i still navigate the underbelly of society with the type of piety and humableness that makes it hard for ppl to believe I'm covered with a numbness that their minds will never encompass

   you can't understand me unless you were raised under the lights cause they ain't want us at nights

   and even though I'm ultra intelligent would you believe it took for me to be imprisoned to know I had rights and even learned I was worth more than the racist vision that an interventionist envisioned for a way to get blacks back to slavery (that's another story)

so anyway back to the inventory we fucked up out here I've survived the land of desolation I'm reaching further than expectation look at what I see ...

    mommy fuckin a nigga named Reggie who blowing loud , ghetto babies crying is the sound daddy not around cause he his step kids daddy now ,cops still on the prowl

grandma face barely smile seems like all she do is scowl .....man I guess that's the face of the mother who loses faith in her only child ,meanwhile every young nigga out here wit a few tats and dreads get a gun and swear he wild right up until a picture of his face is on a t-shirt with the back drop of clouds.... teddy bears all around ...but these are thoughts we think but should never utter out of our mouths but if it's never talked about or spoke on then this continuous heartbreak will keep breaking on and breaking on until we're completely broken and gone .... Mannn the streets don't teach niggas they eat niggas when will y'all understand?

      there's no love in these streets, My heart is screaming and hoping for peace so I'm begging for your attention so I can beg harder for the violence to cease

Kevlar Dreams

They told me they love me , they told me they love me because they knew I wanted to hear it
Then They had the audacity to show me their backs in abandonment because their minds tricked them into believing I would fear it but that only showed that their thought processes couldn't be coherent but what it did make crystal clear and apparent ... it seems to be something in my spirit they didn't inherit so now ive become their target as opposed to helping get my vision into the market ,I was riding for a min but I had to park it ,dead the situation spark it but it's funny how ppl outline situations then get upset cause you decide to chalk it in times past when i was asked I refused to answer ,in hindsight i notice silence only left room for lies and slander to spread like cancer...funny thing is we weren't family since before the crack pipes and back bites leading to fist fights .... how did y'all think that would affect us looking from our kiddie sights ? See ,the sneaky way they get you not to speak up is to accuse you of seeking pity ,right? I know somebody thinking « how he know this shit ? » Silly right? So maybe you'll let me give you some philly advice .... I need you to know it's cool to go ahead and live your life ,do whatever you like ,the bright light of your mornings should not be darkened by the shadows of their nights ,from this day on never let another person's wake up dictate your lay down ... dawg ask about me i been flat leaving these niggas since the playground i AINT never had time to play around , they cut me loose from that prison ..Im on my way now so every time i open my eyes i think I'm gon hit the top any day now my advice is simple FIND SOMETHING YOU BELIEVE IN , PUT YOUR HEART IN ...and stay down

Lemons

   Just like many of you the things I've been through is what makes me think life gave me lemons but the difference is when i came to the comprehension that life gave me lemons , i got on a mission (notice i didn't say competition?) .... soooo now I sell lemon juice,lemon pie,lemon cakes, lemonade and lemon custard .... bitch I'm a hustler ...

   moving how the movers move and shaking like the shakers shake

   what they refuse to give ,we prepared to take ....niggas like us gon live cause we don't break when we go broke , these are just a few of the truest words a real nigga ever spoke ...

You see ,this is what happens when cool kids grow into cool ass adults ... mix dedication wit ambition ,focus on our vision forever we never cared how the haters felt ....we too busy tryna play this fucked UP ass hand these folks done dealt....DIG THIS SHIT

We playing blackjack , but they saying we ain't got rights to our ACES and if we speak up then we viewed as racists..so BASICALLY I can't say how we deprived of foundational basics?

That's not allowed to be said aloud??

     How can you look into the eyes of your child ,naw seriously like how can you expect your kids to be proud of a coward (you upset cause you feel like you aren't ?)quick question HOW DAFUQ AGENT ORANGE WIT THE FREAKY HAIR GET VOTED INTO POWER?? (tell me how we got here , and don't act like you don't know) and please don't expect me not to say something tho , when you come from the mud you get to say whatever the fuck you want cause we grind to get ours, this is just a thought as i blew on some sour one of them late night hours , i really hope y'all dig that this is more than a few words that rhyme , start figuring out how to transform them lemons into limes , I'm telling you y'all better get on y'all type times….. cause these capitalistic ppl damn sure on theirs

Life the walking contradiction....

I'm an orphan/ I am her son
I'm so boring/ I am the epitome of fun
I'm a mean word/ I am a consoling hug
I'm a peaceful Muslim/I am a menacing thug
I'm a man without identity/I am the man in the mirror
I'm just like you/I am like no other
I'm a convicted killer/ I am betrayal's brother
I'm street smart/I am worldly dumb
I'm lavishly rich/I am a dead broke bum
I'm a shooting star/ I am a shattered prism
I'm a rock without wavering position/ I am the life of Shahid.... A walking contradiction

Live From The Snippers Nest

I've noticed most of us are content living these safe lives swimming in this lake of lies , when will you guys realize it's better for us to do more than just survive but to thrive in the sea of entrepreneurial success ,but yet we are still just a little too mercurial in the workplace...

   so on this edition we gon speak of my road to perdition and how it led to me being in a position of knowing the inside sedition of prison and one of the first things I learned about life in the system is that it's a war of attrition ,why do you think the soldiers are so well conditioned ?

   Survival is the mission , you ever been in the hole fishing ? did I mention the whole reason for my learning this method of fishing was cause it was my food these motherfuckers just chose to spit in!? (and this is a long way from home them riflers up there triple dare you to have a sit in ,that shit will quickly transform into a die out, we was trained to ride out MANNNNNN I saw Grizz punch a captain in the face ,broke his nose damn near knocked his eye out , I ain't got shit to lie about

I been in places where we knew the difference between inmates and convicts ,where the truest killers walked around on some truly calm shit

     nowadays y'all be out here screaming GVNG GVNG ÀND STEADY TRYNA CON SHIT actin like y'all quiet storms then quietly calling you Og to calm shit , fake fly niggas stay sneak dissin trying to bomb shit I'm home from prison ,feeling different, tryna CONQUERTHE WORLD im talkin GENGHIS KHAN IN HIS PRIME SHIT

And what's really been on my mind and shit is I wish we all up knew exactly what we were worth and the lack there of is evident in what I see y'all do for a perc and what's worse is how we continue to place ourselves in the dungeons of other ppl 's castles as if we ain't got enough uphill battles topped off with the fact that the words "family"and "hassle" seems to be related extremely closely nowadays,nobody wants work ,yet we all wanna be showered with praise and what's even more despicable is how the only thing in the hood that's predictable is that it's still so unpredictable, so everybody scheming on the minds of those that are dreaming of a better way ....while the minds of those dreaming of a better way are plotting on the getaway, I have an admission, i got an addiction to lavish life livin...German cars, money ,jewels and fast women .... boss is my mindset mixed wit precision and that's probably why I love the foreign engineering ...ride wit me while I'm steering through my mind back to a sad time ....

What's sad you ask?

What's sad is I asked my cellie one day "who got hands ?"
but his response sent me into deep thought ....he said
"Sha niggas don't box and make up, they shoot for nothing leaving niggas on they backs in a box wit makeup " then I started thinking ... what dafuq happened to niggas mixing and shaking hands afterwards without blinking? Now it's like wherever you see drinkin and girls you can expect death ☐ to accompany they all seem to fit quite well comfortably

but we hate to speak of the thug cousin who's now paraplegic your avoidance of him is strategic cause you don't wanna face the reality of being a nigga in the street ...

what y'all fail to realize is real street guys sit around and devise plans to get out of this life sentence of being recognized as gangsters in all homelands yet somehow you weirdos have started to describe this relationship as a romance when in all actuality I've been abducted by the tar and street lights to elude hunger by the dawn's earliest lights and the stress of daytime heartbreaks just add to my stress but I guess I'm just trippin .... yeah I'm just trippin.... but this is Philadelphia, so before I go back outside , let mega ahead and put this clip back in

Mahogany Kisses

Thoughts of sweet mocha caramel chocolate kisses makes me wanna lay her down and give her the business... Our bodies kill time... no witness tho.... She challenges me to see how far I'm willing to go ,cause she's already primed to give it to me whether that be fast or super slow mo ... Little does she know I'm bout to take her on a fantastic voyage ,enticing her senses ,letting her see I meant this it wasn't a mistake nor happenstance ,ay if you're freaky and you know it clap your hands (or something else if the cake is right) all I know is somebody's biscuit is getting baked tonight cause I'm bout to wrestle with the man in the boat until I can see the veins in your throat and when you say "please stop! I can't cope" I will stop ....just long enough to look up and say NOPE! Cause I'm on the attack like I've waged a war on your body ,this a full court press ,making you say confusing things like nonono & yes yes yes .... I never want the less cause the definition of insatiable is when you think you gave me enough I beg for more raising the score my tongue goes on tour all over your body becoming familiar until they are more than mere acquaintances or associates but rather they yearn for each other like fiends and their favorite opiates and we surf each other's wave ,until we take it to the highest point then ride back to earth as it quakes (oh by the way I love the way your ass shakes) you laugh saying I'm the worst and you like that I'm a little perverse but I just smile and say ..... This is why us works....

MY GUYS

Through his joyous tear stained eyes he looks at his guys knowing his rise wouldn't have been attainable except through their hard work and dedication to his vision of what they all would bring to the table and how it would play out they would be mythical,legendary as well as the fables they would spin about these men who walked through the jungle watching each other's six like they were a navy seal team 6 real shit I'm serious tho their hearts were connected they were a real team everybody so busy helping one another nobody has a thought to scheme none of us were named Martin or Luther but these kings had a dream and it involved a whole lot of cream , you gotta know it wasn't the those thoughts of diamonds that made his eyes gleam no, rather it was the comrades he locked into maybe it's the thought even if you think it's bad that if they with him he can die for them before he has to lose any of them but before he would die for any of them he would move correctly and live for them all and look good doing it... don't y'all love takin a trip into the mind of a dude that only knows how to hustle and ball ...but this the thing tho ...y'all really should pay closer attention to the rise because that shit came from the ruins of our ancestors fall

Personal Promises

In pursuit of success one thing is a for sure bet , the first brick is always the hardest to form ,especially when starting out with mud formed into pebbles, they're impressed with the petals on the rose that they seen grow from that concrete ,i ran wit the killers in the big house ,seems my heart is made of concrete, no morals , i was raised by the street , grew up in a home where they was blowing that concrete... my mind is the place where the storm and the calm meet ,my vision & wisdom conquering the world is where my potential & promise meet ,the bank and my account is surely where the commas will meet and I'll never let you down is what I look in the mirror every morning and promise...... me

Poisonous Lies

My heart is dying suffering from an infection of everyone's lying my humanity is crying over the fact that no one seems to be trying anymore and the vultures are picking over the carcass of my love on some sucker shit and the only cure for this condition is finding myself in the position of seeing black males come together on some cousin and brother shit allowing the women to heal the women on some auntie and mother shit because i KNOW our success would change the whole game on some other shit I promise if we support each other no matter what they order we can cover it .... you see ,we all possess a fire those closest either smother it or keep it kindled ...most times the message is sent through their impatience being masked as them just being anxious never understanding that their inactivity is actually our dreams anchors I've always found a profound amount of fascination with those who refuse to help us reach our destinations taking issue with how fast we move in pursuit to it or in our procrastination so I guess as sure as the color blue is blue then I guess this other statement just has to be true too ... PPL DONT KNOW HOW TO MIND THEIR OWN FUCKIN BUSINESS.... if you won't help then surely your critique is hate I'm here for more than mere survival ,but I'm gon let y'all keep doin what y'all do....so go head ....sit,watch, and wait on my hard work ,focus and discipline to make it's loud arrival...its name is success and guess what....we haven't even begun to get started yet!!

Predatory Reflections

Who from amongst you would blame an abandoned child ,raised and nurtured in the wild by snakes who after a while begins to carry their venom ,he's mastered their hunting systems ,he suffers from their symptoms of constant shedding , life's bottom seems to be his bedding ,yet he refuses to believe that this is as good as it's getting ,working from the sun's rising until the setting ....he survives and lives his nine lives mannnnnn this is one cool cat ,in fact ,he's a mammal that's been through more than most can handle ,always thankful his check still hasn't been cancelled everybody wants to see his vision but can't tune into his channel,I'm trying to teach lil sis that all her hate and anger needs to be dismantled and placed on a mantle as a memento of less fortunate years ,what i think it is is I've found a different type of clarity through all my tears maybe this is the reason so much of my advice seems to come out so clear ,I smile as I re-acclimate myself back into my natural habitat of the ghettos because I find that my heart is full of cheer I'm seeing that the beautiful people are still here they just stopped talking cause ...welll.....they heard y'all stopped listening .... too caught up with the shinin and the glistenin ,so while the real jewels were bein given out y'all was missing out on it nowadays you don't even know how to gauge friendships losing money by the bucket fuqn wit kinship.....

I fear humans will continue to lose their humanity trying to solve insanity caused by an insatiable greed in today's world everybody's desires should be fulfilled with speed or then they don't want it , not even if it's an essential need

    I've seen so much fuck shit it's like my heart is under siege I can barely breathe without feeling like I'm being deceived by the shiny lights of lies on other people's tongues ,I just feel so dumb I hate the fact that I can't be numb like all the times ,they said nowadays the world is a pool well i guess i just been swimming ☐ in its lies , breaststroking just hoping to go further and further away so no one ever can say they heard my cries....but then I realize .....It may be that sharing my pain could help of you guys

    o

Pretty Boys, Dirty Fingernails

I'd say I'm a pretty boy wit dirty fingernails / grew up with the mindset of 10 Stringer Bells I'm different different stepped out of prison mixing Fendi wit Chanel rocking stripes on my lapel this swag heavier than uncle L's when he was out here rockin bells and don't get it twisted I'm protected by shells from assault riffles ...real rap ...no mumble... we gon skip the rumble ...these flip and tumble ...knockin pieces off (no stumbles) my boys in the mix ....all gumbo ...y'all niggas the shrimps / we do it big ,,, jumbo ,,,I keep my head low .. that's cause I'm humble .. but like i said I'm the coolest thing since homeboy come through in a bucket kangol i can teach the game from a whole nother angle ...first things first ...stick to being ya self and the one you want gon want you..I skip them and pick they girlfriends to run through like water in Mexico when the squad show up it turn into the flex show ...no Dj ....a quarter won't get you into the game that we play ... so if I knock your head off ain't no replay ain't no EA .. IF YOU REALLY MOVE IN SILENCE ... how could your words be twisted? Only the broke get caught wit the he say , she say .. get in our dreams way and it's gon be a price on your head like eBay have the silent killers catch ya body and remain silent...school of WEBAY.....

This is just a thought that runs through my mindeach every day ... I was raised different from y'all raised different (nod if I'm making sense) I can explain why I am the way I am because of ppl like Haam who wouldn't hesitate with putting in the time to grind me to dust and since he's the type of man that killers could trust... I slow down and hold myself to manners and standards that leave weaker men broken with nothing but understanding as a token, you see... my name don't ring bells it awakens old sleeper cells that got mob ties that go back like crack being moved off of beeper sales ... I come from a long line of pretty boys wit dirty fingernails / political cocaine pipelined prisoners eating glorified slave meals cooked in stingers from prison cells you see I'm what happens when the winner loses but stays focused until he prevails , I'm the seasoning salt to you freaky lil snails (that just means I'll kill you wit taste) but the way y'all setup is setup y'all online giving up tapes while i was trained to ride outside no lights and no brakes move powder balls accumulated from snowflakes i revised that vision sittin in prison upstate came home to a buncha you niggas moving like cupcakes so I focused on myself and now my life on the uptake and if you can't hear what I'm saying now don't worry .... just wait ......y'all know the dope dealers was the smartest in the class we just usually got there late

PROPERTY OF DA GAME

They say I'm crazy ....i say yeah ,crazy like a Fox ......i think they upset because I think so far outside their box that they get confused whenever I tell em I'm aiming for something past that thing they think is the top while in all actuality it isn't even a spot it's actually free moments to enjoy things like children's laughter in the air as it sings or spring's trees blooming even though death is looming and it isn't around the corner anymore it's right here on our doorsteps ... came home to instagram telling em they models so now black babies are aborted ... doctor grab the forceps , y'all niggas ain't tell y'all young bouls stop shooting ? It ain't get close enough for y'all to feel remorse yet? Mentally I'm a giant scoring like wilt representing every fallen soldier killed in the field so I could give a fuck bout how y'all feel they told me to stay down til I come up but I'm drowning ... water from shits creek is steadily filling my lungs up ...and I spit real shit so true niggas love me like new ones new buns and new guns .. pick one ... my presence is heavy like two tons if you black and got a son and don't like the way it's going then do somethin and aim to be righteous remember Money is worthless , time is priceless losing real ones to the streets cause suckers can't stay in their own lane got the game in a crisis , grew up running wit cane like my nickname was O- dog daily running o's off on Randolph goober was the first nigga I met that ran off on the plug twice and live long enough to have a son born twice ....and that's wild cause I know some niggas that would've knocked him down for half price we was young niggas and them old heads was throwing that Montana and we was catching like Rice we ain't dig we was making them rich cause our cash out was nice I ain't lying to say I know some real thoroughbred niggas that was real street bosses who paid the heaviest of cost is redundant they done paid the ultimate prices ... when they say it cost to be the boss lemme tell you what they not telling you : it's never the money cost because if you see how money is made and lost you'd then wonder what the price is and I'd say "youngin the streets are a bloody revenue "... so when they take their cut it sits you down & teaches you a pain you never knew , mannnnn don't mind me, what the fuck i ever knew?i learned from mistakes , cleansing through the filth made me better too , anyway what I'm tryna tell you is consequences to action will have you laid up learning prison living so I'm here to advise you .....please , matter of fact I'm begging,I'm begging real life begging think twice bout this life you getting into

SAVAGE'S PASSAGE

      Ppl be saying "Sha , you got it all together " i be thinking "hardly" but oddly these thoughts of Garvey is what helps keep me sane in a world seeming to have gon insane , every time I look up another black leader getting caught wit their hands in the cookie jar I'm not judging but watching from afar it seems your leaders are chasing fame meanwhile Harriette's blood pumps through his veins Malcom's ferocity is what powers this brain Martin's cool demeanor and leadership is what covers his frame ... Nat Turner's resolve is what flows through his arteries yeah live free or die free that's truly what's at the heart of me ,they listened and said my word play is true artistry then , then remarkably told me they couldn't figure out a way to market me , the industry paying your favorite rappers to say they went to the school of hard knocks and since it look like all y'all lost y'all common sense and got into buying lies I guess that's cool or what not but you see I grew up as a professor on small blocks yeah a drug dealing child prodigy and so smart probably Harvard would be honored to be dishonorably discharging me the lack of effort when it comes to being black fathers is what's been bothering me ...you see we was pushed out the house forced to choose from the most despicable of routes just tryna keep a lil food in our mouths ...i just done a prison sentence so long in them state browns that the state brown faded came home to love ,no help ,and no support and that's ok IM still unfaded THIS IS THE DEFINITION OF NIGGA WE MADE IT ... but i got a question? I just gotta know ,who tricked y'all into making the black woman the one so easily degraded? My mindset is nothing to play wit y'all niggas is foul Disgusted with ya flagrance ..... I gotta say this you can't be a real nigga and still sign them ppl statements I could give a fuck about being your new favorite, im more concerned wit the fact that y'all cats can't seem to keep these kids out the streets, like you don't understand it's a reason they made them pavements , the reaper out here and he don't accept his blood payment in installments... just a lil advice from a nigga grew up in life lawless ,ducking them lawmen .... I need you to think bout this next time you say them streets is a callin .... i can tell you from personal experience....the scent of death is appalling

Seaside shells

      She's seductive in a way that she only knows...... her style works me purposely and my mouth wants to meet her personally our bodies meet until I'm so entrenched in her scent and she's covered in my smells and we're so comfy that we're officially out of shells and she thinks it can't get better but it does and we make eachother feel the type of affection that's more geared towards reflections of what we think of ourselves I hear her getting turned on by my presence she wants me with or without the gifts and presents I want to make her love come down But I must first prove that the king is fit to wear the crown in her kingdom.......2b cont.

Self-Reflection Check-In

It was all good while we were young and wild
    until it was time to stand trial (alone) .... fast forward to now .... I'm home completely grown finding myself in a state of perplexion asking myself this question through a poem .....What did being a "real nigga" ever get me? Turned on ,lied on , slandered, shot up and left for ☐ dead ... it's crazy cause the tally still being added up to determine if it was more of my blood or my tears that's been shed,I been fucked up , i ain't gon lie if you play the game long enough you bound to luck up and I'm a gangster through and through but i been stuck up, i got caught in that system but I've done more than survived the shit ..I've gained wisdom ,patience and a healthy dose of humility , which gives me the ability to face a reptile with a certain type of civility... you see , Im what happens when confidence and ambition have a conference with your conscience ,this type of drive doesn't need sponsors and you can look into my eyes and tell that I was raised by real life monsters ,Gun totin cocoa house sponsors but my mind is Akon it brightens up neighborhoods like it's free electricity I'm tryna help youthful ppl understand life and it's complexity

    Yet it seems as if my elders are pressed to be viewing me according to my past crimes never mind how I heal their babies minds with something as simple as a little attention and time

    if efforts were selected they'd find that eclecticism is what will brighten our star releasing the prism letting us loose from this mental prison we been in

    but y'all too busy trying to look rich wealth and stability should be our focus re ride for everybody cause but ours SLOW DOWN one of the first things that will be hard to ignore is the vultures because they keep themselves so close to our existence only really just to say they saw when we were once inconsistent inside of everything we ever seek to build from our constant consistence....

    Would y'all believe it's actually Ppl out here that say I'm acting exclusivey ..... i know for a fact it's cause I won't allow em close enough to start using me.... you know the type : walk right in and tell you EVERYTHING THEY THINK YOU SHOULD BE DOIN WIT YOUR LIFE .... whole time the, snakes be side eyeing your bread tryna figure out how to steal a slice so my advice is simple..make ppl earn friendship nowadays because they don't expect friendship they give you hassle for standing up for self because they truly expect obedience... but I'm a different type of baker i make my bread from scratch so naturally i got the audacity to turn around and ask welllllllll where were y'all asses at when it was time for me to gather the ingredients ?

Silent Tears?

I know pain personally ,my strength refuses to let the tears fall from my eye...
    I'm prepared to live life I'm not just waiting on my turn to die ...
And this is strange since life's cruel lashes have left my heart covered in gashes ...
Your mind is now saturated in my thought's gasses....my speech is the matches,
   I'm prepared to cause an inferno but this isn't your concern tho
    my intelligence will set the world on fire and you just wanna watch it burn yo.....
    I can control my tongue no matter how mad I get which makes my silence so inadequately adequate ....
See , I'm good being lonely
   I am the only one that knows me ....
    an unlovable soul is what the world's mirror has shown me ,to the point that my heart is sick it's losing love's weight it's bony and the cause is most of the ppl entrusted to love me have been phony ... Real life fakes all the way across the board snakes prepared to do what it takes to ruin me for reasons still unknown to me,   They've disowned love's land and treason has been shown
  luckily or should I say fortunately I'm grown
so I can make it on my own ,allowing you to do you ,while I do me in my lonely lil zone ....
   I'm really not mad or angry ,not even a lil upset ....just sad wondering how bad does it get before the best comes wondering why the worst stuff seems to happen to the best ones

Sophisticated Psycho

Would you be offended if every person you ever befriended found it shocking because your speech and vocabulary are made up of the best meanings of diversity and you know they're only shocked because you come from a background full of adversity and didn't attend their university cause you were too busy trying to survive life personally? I believe understanding is instrumental to peace , yet I deem everybody to have become a lil too judgmental to the point that gavels should be a number one seller around Christmas (it's crazy cause y'all won't openly admit this) but it's on all y'all wish lists.....so here's my response , you're all hypocrites and the reason I say this is because there's been more than one instance where the public's outrage showed the same constant inconsistence in it's persistence for justice ,it's to the point that we won't even discuss this , cause it disgusts us....I mean I listen to ppl talk and their words don't match their walk, like why do we ignore the things that we should abhor, but I won't say a name cause the cops will be here to chalk that relationship if I should ever tell em how fucked up they are as a person , so I sit back and watch em worsen , I'm determined not to get involved because I've evolved into something their minds can't fathom but as sure as you hear my speech know this ... they'll kill him if they can't have em ... at some point I'll have the type of paper to give you more than a microcosm of my thought process I'm an ever evolving growth project and i just need you to be patient you're now locked in watching me go through the process of leading us directly towards progress

As I Rise Foreword

As I wrote "As I rise" I thought of all the times I've failed ,of all the times I've suffered setbacks and how I felt when I was down ,stuck thinking of how to fight back and it made me remember that feeling of determination in my stomach.

I knew that I was destined for greatness or at least more than what I was doing or receiving in the world so I began to use my hard points as reflections of my strength and began to embrace those moments and flourish under those circumstances.

A-When I wrote as I rise,I did so intelligently never knowing that it was already written by the late great Maya Angelou so eloquently and you have to believe me when I say I have never read or even picked up a poetry book or piece of poetry until I began to write because again where I come from we just don't do that so it's ironic that I'm now a published poet (I don't view myself that way though) remember that in order to rise you will have to have been down and the strength you show is what will determine how you're viewed by the world now ....so RISE

As I Rise

We all have choices.... We all have voices....
My mind is uncharted territory like the third triangle of the Bermudas, since childhood 100 judas have been part of my life , determined to impair my vision ,blur my sight and ruin my life ... Yet still I RISE!!!
I've been beaten, abused, mistreated and mislead ....taught the wrong truths but I bought it cause the best future commander understands the size of the boots he's putting on his troops I been shot and I've done the shootings , pushed crack cocaine.... hood polluting but that was just love in disguise jolt doing something i now today despise .... Yet still I RISE!!!!
I've been stripped out and embarrassed broken down to my lowest denominations my lowest compound my lowest components and they still don't understand why the man in the mirror is my biggest opponent cause my vision is what I see , I figure to own it ...but these bars bring about impatient sighs ..... Yet still I RISE!!!!!
Freedom has been purchased with 15 long years of humiliation and degradation but I'm prepared for graduation, my family's awaitin my return(at least I thought)but it was just like Notorious B.i.g. said IT WAS ALL A DREAM
cause the scheme was on and the fix was in ...sooooo no ticker tape parade or keys to the city? Just a few fake hugs and a bunch of pity, look at the crown of

thorns they've placed upon the head of young street sire laughed at and ridiculed until he rises from the ashes ...now pay closer attention as their teeth gnashes for surely they hope he's more Icarus than Phoenix   but I say to those viewers of despise " please continue to pray for my demise...... but in the meantime WATCH AS I RISE!!!!!!!!!

Tales from a lost soul

      Sometimes in the middle of chasing commas, I slow down and go down north and kick it wit the young piranhas chopping it up over the sweet smells of marijuana i remind em to move with character and honor i tell em stand for something cause fake niggas dying and killing over personas i remind em that street niggas don't get karma they get 100 shells thrown at their body armor this some advice one time from a nigga fresh off the frontlines I'm home from prison and i want mines so it's always grind time so i move in my own lil world careful who i let into my dimension cause these sucker niiggas acting up doing anything for attention got the hood hotter than sunshine, shooting blindly catching bodies , fake tough guys really aspire to be the next Gotti but getting cuffed and been going out like Sammy that's the definition of the double whammy and that's what I mean when I say YOU NIGGAS ON SOME BULL SHIT!!! Y'all so lazy y'all refuse to do homework so any info is cool if it's coming from a person standing on a pulpit and that's the type of stuff that has My brain itching... my mind twitching ....cause it must be a glitch in y'all gaming system ...don't y'all see the misguided aggression and anger is only feeding into a racial vision ? I feel like sitting in prison didn't leave me behind .....it excelled me past y'all by light years .... fucked me up to find out y'all out here living Dr King's nightmares and cementing Willie Lynch's dream ... talkin bout y'all all bout that cream talkin bout have you ever danced wit the devil under pale moonlight ? I'm asking have you ever looked up and wondered what the fuck the moon even look like cause you been in prison so long you wonder if ppl even remember if you alive and kicking take your mind back to then and you'll notice these the same vultures tryna fit in now that you home and they heard you back in the kitchen.... pay attention ....cause these the same type of niggas that'll have your front and back doors kicked in ... don't wait til your man got it pointed to the back of your head to wish you listened

Televised Revolution

Hmmmmm..... Truth is ,you're weak.. not sufficient , intelligence department you're deficient, but when it comes to bad decision making you're quite proficient ..... You see, I hate to be the one that's gotta look you in the eyes and tell you that you won't survive the evolution of the thinking guys ...while my old heads were telling them the revolution wouldn't be televised your old heads told you guys that yall some REAL NIGGAS and that's cool and what not but the only problem with that is now you weirdos running around acting like REAL...NIGGERS... And what I mean is your idiocy is the policy ,while intelligence is placed on a shelf , y'all throwing away y'all futures and just so you can enhance another mans wealth ...you know like 300 dollar belts ,catching new charges cause you been havin visions of how many bitches you gon pull when you pull up in one of dem there Hellcat Chargers doin all types of stupid shit like killers don't kill ppl and go on bout they day unbothered and this is the reason so many kids don't have fathers cause sadly you'd rather hear a whore call you daddy over your offspring ? you lost yourself caught up in what you think the streets are offering .... What happened to original thinking? .... I guess y'all forgot how to use your minds to get to the bank and let your ideas milk it , never look for the handout good niggas receive their help as they build it ...i heard kings had dreams but them folks implanted a scheme & placed drugs in between in pursuit of small cream had some REAL NIGGAS slide thru and did a drive by on some hatin shit and killed it killed it killed it .... this is where the vision begins and doubt ends….. time to separate the boys from the men ....so last question REAL NIGGA you out or you in ???

The Art of Gem Polishing

I feel like somebody is out here truly working the Willie Lynch plan amongst black folks , that thing is like the Devil's Bible , one of the most base concepts for this plan to be successful against black ppl is separating the men from the women and one of the for sure ways is make her think he can't provide for her and hopefully just hopefully he'll believe it and she will give up on him.... problem with their theory is he's began to believe he's worthless and yet she still won't give up on him and the epidemic is even worse than thought with the black man because he's not only lost the value of his own worth he has also lost the value in the one person who can save him from himself and that's the BLACK WOMAN , he makes songs so degrading about her but his sentiment is clear that he loves her but he also refuses to grow and show her that he is willing and determined to build a future and foundation with her instead he grows Willie Lynch's army by luring the black woman into serious relationships that he has no intentions of taking seriously as he is to busy trying to figure out a way to show her how worthless she is to him , and I know this will be met with pushback but I push back harder and my statement is true because if they were meeting women upon patience, understanding, support and growth then they would surely be meeting upon love. The love I speak of is the love every person should naturally have for other ppl , a few examples such as how we would all agree Latino men will die and kill for their women , white ppl wrote THE WHOLE BOOK OF RULES to protect their women , Asian men wont even let outsiders close enough to learn the dynamics of their man/woman relationships.... so my question is what does the black woman get from the black man ? So where is this love the black man should have for the black woman ? Like I said in the beginning he's lost sight of the value in himself so naturally he's lost sight of all value of her .... he feels more comfortable calling her his bitch than his queen because he can't see that he's a king you see, I'm not going to make statements without proofs readily available, the plan is to rebuild ourselves and stop begging for help , but there can't be a plan thought to be successful if we don't understand that we don't need anybody else's help ,

the only help we need is the help of the most powerful ppl on the planet , The Black Woman

The New Real

It's a war goin on outside no blacks safe from ,,,domestic terror been a real threat, white ppl y'all think it's time to take white ppl guns yet ? And y'all real niggas is proving to be real fake ones cause how black women & children ain't safe from the burn of y'all ray guns ? y'all minds been bleached my nigga   can't understand this ? 9 times outta 10 you already mentally outta reach my nigga ain't shit in them streets but rats , snakes and a couple raw broads ,Our expectation of yall was to never go raw dawg my nigga but y'all dummies done slipped up , went and sold y'all souls for designer drugs and clothes … ohh noooo he hot on the scene but when the heaters got drawn ..guess who heat just froze? And when the sirens ring and the cuffs get clinked ,he transforms into fresh laundry the way the heat helps him easily fold ,but internet pages see him scream he's ten toes ,forces me to stare into the windows of his soul and let em know they sentence by the decade nowadays lil broyou ready to do ten of those now?! Betrayal is evident cause how many times we seen that it fuck round and be a nigga main man name as the D.A's first piece of evidence so where the common sense @ my Nigga ? y'all dropping each other over small dug knots on smaller drug blocks broke niggas got more bullets in the chop than paper in they pockets calling each other opps and what not... dying in the field obsessed wit invisible commas ,this goofy shit got me ready to Malcolm X flex on y'all pale faced personas them scars on my body probably tell the story of a killer whale swimming wit snake minded piranhas my presence is the essence and reminder of a time when black folk were much kinder and the men were built on things like character,unity and honor real life Wakanda kinda ,nowadays y'all niggas wanna be the biggest snakes shit look weird like pythons attempting to swallow anacondas aaaaaaand Trust and believe If I say anything bout you freaks and geeks personally I bet you already heard it at the tip of your beak y'all actions show that y'all weak ol half assed gangsters, full time wanksters we all street learned to sharpen our teeth on all beef definition of my success is we all eat the fruits of our labor got success tasting ripe type sweet we took the sci thoroughbred route y'all out here taking the snake your man crumble and take the stand route we got it out the mud so fair ones the only thing we readily handout can't respect any man out here head down and hand out I'm really a street nigga get spicy and watch how fast them cans come out ,survivalist advice never allow the same cat to burn you twice because that type of deception will have you grabbing your weapon getting to stepping soon as you see him now you marrying the game throwing that shit at em like rice at the reception I'm tryna teach you a lesson lil homie your presence is a blessing they trying to get you missing before you complete your mission I can give you advice in the flyest ways but only your limbs will show if you truly did hear it or just a nigga nodding your head and listening ....I'm the pressure it's time to either bust pipes or you niggas gon start glistening

Thoughts of Huey

Listennnnn you gotta pay attention mannnnnn , cause I swear these niggas out here moving they hands all freely like they ain't Edward scissorhands himself you see, I built my life off of my mind's visual plans , mixed my ambition and dedication and it's steadily leading me to the wealth , I didn't
come to regurgitate our issues,I'm trying to explain a solution first things first,we gotta stop putting violence in the air ,we trained to kill one another through the music (that shit is toxic pollution) I wanna say peace to the kings and queens tryna build through separate institutions i need black kids to stop tryna be Bill gates and try to be a mansa musa but like Nip said "this ain't the weirdo rap you motherfuckers used to"...we lookin like The X clan in this minivan and them choppers protect the brother man like child soldiers imported from the motherland ..I had high hopes for the youngins but it looks like the devil had other plans , i done seen oxymoronic scenes play out daily in my lifetime ....they ciphoned my dreams to the prisons through cocaine pipelines ...pay attention cuz cause these folks sneakier than black ants on black rocks moving at nighttime so watch out cause they'll trick you ....stealing the light out your bulb and selling it back to you saying it's a new shine , don't believe me? I've watched it done at least a half million times bro

Turn Down For What

We're nobodies .....
seriously
our lack of intelligence has us lacking in relevance....
   or should I say rather ,the lack in action upon the intelligence we gather has us looking like new school buffoons and that even to old school coins ..... I'm tired of hearing the same ever evolving statements of "free my folks" & "gone too soons"
   never mind how we watch these heartless goons destroy and pillage....
what ever happened to simple statements like "it takes a village to raise a child" ....
    Ask yourself ,if after a while we were to band together and stand together funneling money back into our community showing a different type of unity
   Do you suppose guys would still be dying in chokeholds?
 Do you think the cops would think twice before filling unarmed college bound kids with multiple shots?
But you see ,when the parents absence is apparent the answer is clear to the so called rhetorical question of "turn down for what?"
TURN DOWN FOR THE KIDS

TURN DOWN FOR MORALS
TURN DOWN FOR THE FUTURE
TURN DOWN FOR THE WHAT IS VERSUS THE WHAT WILL BE ,FOR WHAT YOU DON'T SEE AND WHAT YOU DON'T WANNA BE
   TURN DOWN BECAUSE IT WILL BE OUR DEMISE....
   TURN DOWN BECAUSE IF WE CONTINUE TO TURN UP…...

OUR BABIES WON'T SURVIVE

Wealthy Mindset

When I get with her it's something my mind can barely handle ,especially when I walk in the bedroom and see she done lit that candle ... I know I'm bout to get handled matter of fact all the rest of today's plans have just been canceled

  I read her body only as a poets love letter and she informs me that I better continue to have the same type of energy or she will instantly turn into nothing more than a empty lovers mystery inside my hearts long history of heartbreak , our chemistry is something we refuse to allow the public to partake in,

    passion caused my love to seek out her lonely island, never suffering through awkward silence, i heard her tears hitting my t shirt even as we were standing there still smiling at first encounters and all of these beautiful words could only amount to a mans being trapped in the war fields of love and even when I'm down to my very last bucks ,it's in her presence that I feel like daddy war bucks so when I get mad and say I don't care just remember ....I still give a few hard fucks

WORLDLY COLLISIONS

   Guess what ?
What?
   I was wrong you was right ,my heart went for the banana in the tailpipe twice in the same life ...
    yup somebody came out the darkness and spit on my light ...so now this is the part of the poem where he explains how nobody really knows em and how he can't see why nobody will ever be right in his life ,right? NOPE This is the part where Noah closed off his ark and prepared to depart
     there's a different spark in his heart he's headed somewhere off of everybody's chart
And on this ride there's no need to hear a smart retort or an undercover report of how I'll be loved one day or how I'm sure to be forgiven for this certaint type of living that they ingrained into my mind like religion
    but after I went to prison they changed their living and inevitably my exit from the DOC caused a different type of entrance into their remembrance
   and as I tried to gain their interest it wasn't until I left and really gave everything into my best interest

which was self invest and it wasn't until I started to monetarily show some interest did they take interest in my existence so now use your imagination to picture my exasperation in noticing my daughters are not even acknowledged my babies happiness keeps my heart polished like sterling silverware so after i dry they eyes and wipe my tears i pray i convey this here crystal clear...
we not around
Im not for the repetitive abuse labeled as familial ties that are more like different versions of people's lies placed in their children's minds cause you motherfuckers don't know how to properly spend time finding a grind to leave a legacy living pleasantly ,well I do and I'm gon provide whatever for mine

   This is it...our relationship has reached its conclusion time for more of my reclusion ...I'm gon need a large order of y'all ignoring this loud success the same way y'all ignored years of her abusing and please hold the slander ...the problem is I don't know if ppl understand that these aren't just words I gather and bend to create a trend .....naw these are my feelings and for this thought there is no slick way to end ....because well.... it's the end